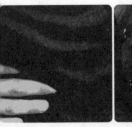

CURRICULUM

LEADER'S GUIDE

WHAT DO YOU WANT?

UNDERSTANDING GOD'S WILL

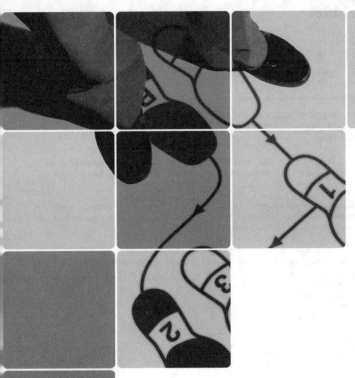

Youth Specialties

ZONDERVAN™

GRAND RAPIDS, MICHIGAN 49530 USA

Youth Specialties

What Do You Want? Leader's Guide
Copyright © 2004 by Youth Specialties

Youth Specialties Books, 300 South Pierce Street, El Cajon, CA 92020, are published by Zondervan, 5300 Patterson Aveune SE, Grand Rapids, MI 49530

Editorial direction by Dave Urbanski
Edited by Kristi Robison
Proofread by Laura Gross and Janie Wilkerson
Designed by Proxy

Printed in the United States of America

06 07 08 09 / CH / 10 9 8 7 6 5 4 3 2

HIGHWAY VISUAL CURRICULUM

Volume Four

WHAT DO YOU WANT?

Introduction

Welcome to Youth Specialties and Highway Video.

Unlike many teaching tools, Highway Video does not presume to tell you what message to communicate to your flock. Instead, it is designed to be a flexible tool you can use to work with whatever message, purpose, and age level you have. Everything from announcements and teaching moments to benedictions, this material can be used with every age level—from middle school kids on up—and for just about any group size and church style.

But we don't want to leave you hanging.

In this booklet we've provided ideas for a variety of possible ways you can use each film clip. We've also included a lesson plan or two for you to check out and plug in wherever you feel it's appropriate. The lessons written for middle school students are short and action-filled. Those written for high school groups are longer with less action but more abstract thinking.

Our lesson plans even have downloadable, reproducible talksheets and other activity resources. You can download them for free off this Web site:

www.YouthSpecialties.com/store/downloads
code word: highway 4

To indicate each possible option for using a particular film clip, we've created a Signpost icon. This symbol designates a new path of teaching or communication for the video segment. With just a glance you'll be able to access a wide expanse of alternatives for using each video clip with your group.

Please feel free to manipulate the video in whatever way works best for your purposes.

For example, you may only want to show a portion of the video. Or you may decide that your group should view the clip more than once, maybe showing it to them a second time after you've explored the subject—just as a reminder.

You may download the video into your computer video editing program and clip the time, add a trailer, insert some Scripture, or use whatever devices you have at your disposal that will help you communicate the point of your lesson or message.

Look for **Production Notes** and its icon to get behind-the-scenes comments from the producers.

For a couple of the Signposts we have gone ahead and mapped out lesson plans for youth groups that support a particular teaching idea inspired from the film clip. Remember, the talksheet resources for these lessons are integrated in these texts, but they can be downloaded and customized for your use free of charge at
**www.YouthSpecialties.com/store/downloads
code word: highway 4**

 **Alternate Routes**

 General Church Use

Looking for a great illustration on the frustration of legalism? Grab this DVD clip and show it as an example of how legalism trips us up, while being led and empowered by the Holy Spirit sets us free to let God guide our steps. Don't forget to let your group know that at one point in the story, the subject finally understands what he *could* become.

 Emergent Ministries

Slot this film clip anyplace it works best for you. Set up the clip by projecting or reading Acts 17:28—"'For in him we live and move and have our being'"—before showing it.

 Small Group

Focus: We are to be people led by the Holy Spirit.

Biblical basis: Romans 7:6; Luke 11:46; Acts 17:28; Psalm 37:31

Stuff you need: *Step By Step* video, discussion questions, Bibles

Getting Started

Ask your students to tell what is meant by the expressions "the spirit of the law" and "the letter of the law." Ask them to give examples, if they can come up with them. After your group has had a chance to give their feedback, transition to the

Bible study by saying something like this:

> **These two terms are actually based on something the apostle Paul wrote to the church in Rome. Let's take a closer look at the original meaning and how that plays out for us in everyday life.**

 Bible Study

Read the following passage to your group:

> But now we have been released from the law, for we died with Christ, and we are no longer captive to its power. Now we can really serve God, not in the old way by obeying the letter of the law, but in the new way, by the Spirit. (Romans 7:6, NLT)

Ask—

* What is the "law" that Paul is referring to in this passage?

* Can you think of anything Jesus said to the religious leaders about the rules and regulations they imposed on people? (See Luke 11:46.)

* Can you think of any "rules" that Christians are asked to obey in some church communities that, as far as you can figure, are not taught clearly in the Bible?

* What does having to follow a heap of rules and regulations do to a typical person?

Transition to the film clip by saying something like this:

> **I would like to show you a short film clip that uses dance steps as a metaphor for what we are discussing today. Let's watch the film clip and then discuss the meaning hidden just beneath the surface.**

▶ *Step By Step* Film Clip

Show *Step By Step*. After the film clip is finished, ask your group questions such as—

* What did all the dance steps on the floor represent?

* What happened as the dancer tried to follow all the steps?

* A single pair of footprints appeared—whom do you think they're supposed to belong to?

* When the dancer (seeing himself for what he could be) stepped into those footprints, what happened to him?

* What was different about his dance after his encounter with the new footprints?

* What do the differences between the two dances mean for us in everyday life?

Read Acts 17:28 to your students and ask them how this verse might relate to the theme of the film they have seen.

Transition to the Wrap Up by saying something like this:

> **Naturally, people make rules because they fear that if we allow them to be led by the Spirit, they will end up doing all kinds of nutty or self-serving things. But**

balance is the secret. The Bible is God's book of guidance for believers, but when we start adding stuff to it or drawing out laws and regulations that aren't there, we can really frustrate people who want to follow Christ. Let's take a moment and see if we can come up with a clear way of thinking to allow God to move in us and through us without being trapped by a load of silly rules.

Wrap Up

Ask your group to brainstorm an answer to the question—How do I let God guide my steps? (See Psalm 37:31 for some help with this question.) Share and close in prayer.

 Middle School

Focus: Rules don't get you there.

Biblical basis: Ephesians 2:8-9

Stuff you need: Twister game, *Step By Step* video, Bibles, large sheet of newsprint, and markers

Getting Started

Have a few volunteers come up and play a game of "Prison Twister." Here's how it works: Using a Twister game, tell your students that if they fail to get their hands or feet on the right color, they're out of the game and condemned to life in prison. Ask the students who are watching to pick the person they think will win—because their own fate is tied to that individual. If a participant loses and goes to prison for life, then the spectator who chose that person goes right along with him. (This encourages more cheering.)

After the game ask or point out to your kids:

> Have you ever noticed that some religions are kind of like Twister—they make their followers go through contortions in order to find heaven? Can you think of an example? Sometimes Christians can make following Christ so hard, with all kinds of silly rules and regulations, that living the Christian life can feel like playing a game of Twister.

Transition to the movie clip by saying something like this:

> **Let's take a look at the same idea, only instead of people playing Twister, it's a guy trying to follow footprints on the floor in order to learn a dance step. As you watch this film, notice when he gets the idea that there must be a better way than getting tangled up by following the complicated steps—he actually can imagine what he might be like if he just moved with the Spirit.**

▶ *Step By Step* Film Clip

Show the film clip. Keep in mind that for some kids this clip may be a bit abstract, and you may need to explain what is going on and the symbolism in it. For instance:

> * The dancer starts out excited but gets more and more frustrated as the steps get more and more complex, just as many Christians find their excitement turned off

when they run into people who want to make
faith more difficult by heaping on legalism
and rules that aren't found in the Bible.

* Finally, two simple footprints appear—the
footprints of Christ. When the dancer steps
into them, he is empowered to dance. This is
a wonderful description of what God does
inside us if we seek to follow his simple lead.

* Note that the dancer sees *himself* dancing.
This shows that he's getting the picture of
what *could* be—then he can make the
choice to keep the frustration going or dance
in freedom.

 ## Bible Study

Ask your kids to open their Bibles to Ephesians
2:8-9 and take a minute to commit these verses to
memory. Then ask your students what they think
the passage means. Discuss briefly the whole idea
of works and grace and how works are kind of like
the dance steps that someone lays out for you to
follow, while grace is kind of like allowing God to
dance through you.

Break the students into groups of four or five and
ask the groups to come up with a simple, one-sen-
tence explanation of how to live as a Christian.
The sentence should be one they could share with
someone who's afraid that becoming a Christian
means following a pile of twisting rules. Ask them
to share what they have written.

Wrap Up

On a large sheet of newsprint, have your students
draw a diagram of the "dance steps" it takes to

follow Jesus without the frustration of legalism, rules, and having to work your way to heaven. Ask them to label their dance steps so they're clear. If your group has been paying attention, they should come up with some very simple steps such as— "Trust Christ" or "Have faith." Close in prayer.

 High School

Focus: Our relationship with Christ is not based on keeping rules but on enjoying God's grace and presence in our lives.

Biblical basis: 1 Peter 2:13-14; Luke 11:37-46; Matthew 12:1-14; Matthew 15:1-3; Ephesians 2:8-9; Acts 17:28

Stuff you need: copies of *Step By Step* Talksheets (optional); paper; pencils; masking tape; two containers; a large screen, projector, PlayStation, and dance video game (optional); Bibles; digital camera (optional); *Dance Steps* video

Getting Started

Idea #1: Start by reading the following Scripture to your group:

> Submit yourselves for the Lord's sake to every authority instituted among men: whether to the king, as the supreme authority, or to governors, who are sent by him to punish those who do wrong and to commend those who do right. (1 Peter 2:13-14)

Ask your students if, based on the passage you just read, they think they should obey the laws that governments set down. (Most will say "sure," as long as the laws don't go against God's instructions.) Now read some of the following *true* laws and statutes found across America. You can also pass out copies of the "It's the Law!" talksheet and let the students read the laws for themselves.

(This page can be downloaded from the Web site for this book: www.YouthSpecialties.com/store/downloads; code: highway 4.)

"It's the Law!" Talksheet

* A 200-pound woman in Gurnee, Illinois, may not ride a horse in shorts.

* In the state of Washington, it is illegal to pretend that your folks are rich.

* In New York, blind men are forbidden to drive automobiles.

* In San Francisco it is illegal to wipe down your car with used underwear.

* In Omaha, Nebraska, it is illegal to shave a man's chest.

* In Rochester, Michigan, anyone wanting to go swimming is supposed to have his or her bathing suit inspected by the police.

* If you have a pony in Vermont, don't paint it! You can get arrested.

* In Tuscumbia, Alabama, you are not allowed to have more than eight rabbits living on the same block.

Taken from *Loony Laws & Silly Statutes* by Sheryl Lindsell-Roberts, Sterling Publishing, 1994.

After you (or your students) have read them, ask if they think these laws should be obeyed. Why or why not? Ask—

* What would your life be like if you tried to obey every silly rule on the books in some cities?

* Do any of these laws go against God's instructions? If no, then why not obey them?

* Do you think anyone should go to jail if they were to break laws such as these? Why or why not?

Transition to the Bible study by saying something like this:

While God has laws that humans shouldn't break, the religious leaders during the time of Christ interpreted many of those laws and added a bunch of new ones. Let's take a brief look at the interaction Jesus had with these religious leaders.

Idea #2: Before your session, put a piece of masking tape on the ground to serve as the starting line of a race. Give two slips of paper and a pencil to each student. Ask them to write any one of the following instructions, or their own similar instruction, on each piece:

TAKE ONE STEP FORWARD.

TAKE ONE STEP BACKWARD.

SPIN IN A CIRCLE.

TURN SIDEWAYS.

TAKE TWO STEPS FORWARD.

HOP UP AND DOWN.

Collect all the slips of paper, divide them into two piles, and put each pile into a hat or bowl or box—whatever you have handy. Ask for two volunteers who will race each other from the starting line—but they must follow the instructions you give them. Once the race has begun, in turn, pull out a slip of paper from each contestant's container and read aloud what the contestant is to do. Chances are this race won't go far. In fact, there might not even be a winner. When you run out of slips of paper, the race is over and the student who has made it the farthest is the winner.

Transition to the Bible study by saying something like this:

> **This silly game is really designed to be a bit of a parable about how frustrating life can be when we bind ourselves with rules and regulations that don't take us anywhere. Let's take a closer look at how this can happen to Christians.**

Idea #3: If your room is set up with a large screen and projection unit, hook up a PlayStation, borrow one of those crazy dancing video games (you know, the ones that come with the mat that shows where to put your feet), and have a short contest to see who can last the longest when the program is cranked up to expert level.

Transition to the Bible study by saying something like this:

> **Imagine that your eternal life is based on how well you did at this dance game! Well, the Pharisees—and even some Christians today—laid out some pretty**

tough steps to follow and put a real burden on people who were trying to nurture their relationships with God, which is actually created to be full of joy. Let's take a closer look at what happened.

Bible Study

Idea #1: Divide your students into groups of four to six and assign each group one of the following activities (and make sure to give them the needed materials to do so):

* Ask at least one group to read Luke 11:37-46 and prepare a short newspaper article—from that historical time period—about the verbal roughing up Jesus gave to the Pharisees. Ask them to create a headline for their article and to make sure they've reported on the core of the message Jesus was trying to get across.

* Ask another group to read Matthew 12:1-14 and to create a series of still photos (this can be done as drawings or by using a digital camera and acting out the parts) to show what took place there.

* Assign another group Matthew 15:1-3 and ask them to create a health report that the Pharisees might have filed against Jesus for this offense.

When your students are finished, pull everyone together and have them share their projects. Ask—

* What were the religious leaders having a hard time with in these passages?

* Do you think their rules were important? Why or why not?

* Sum up the attitude of Jesus toward the rules of the Pharisees.

* Can you think of any rules in the church today that are as narrow or silly as some of the ones we've been looking at?

* Why do you think they have those rules?

Transition to the film clip by saying something like this:

I would like to show you a short movie that deals with the frustration that comes from legalism—or following rules that people have invented—but watch carefully and see if you can spot what would allow for freedom from those things that so easily discourage us.

▶ *Step By Step* **Film Clip**

Show the *Dance Steps* film clip and then discuss it by asking a few questions such as:

* What do you think the dance symbolizes?

* What do you think the complex footprints symbolize?

* What happened as the dance progresses?

* Suddenly, two simple footprints appeared. Any thoughts on what they might represent?

* For a moment the dancer sees what he *could* be when he steps into the place where God can animate him. What is the message to us here?

Idea #2: Pass out blank pieces of paper and pencils to your students. Then, after sharing the following instructions, show the *Dance Steps* film clip.

Tell your students:—

As you watch this short film clip, I want you to think really hard about the meaning of what you are seeing and write down what you think is the theme of this movie.

Play the movie and give your students a chance to write their conclusions. Ask for some to share what they've come up with.

For the sake of all your students, clarify the meaning of the film by telling your whole group something like this:

What we saw was a little parable about how easy it is to lose the joy of our relationship with God by getting tangled up in the rules and expectations that others lay down for us. It demonstrates that God wants us to break away and put simple trust in him to empower and guide us.

Direct your students to the interaction between Jesus and the Pharisees in Luke 11:37-54. Hand out copies of the "Step in the Right Direction" talksheet. (This talksheet can be downloaded from the Web site for this book: www.YouthSpecialties.com/store/downloads; code: highway 4.) Ask them to get into pairs, read the passage, and then inside the shoeprint outlines on the talksheet, they should write down some of the legalistic things the religious leaders did or required people to do, as well as any legalistic things some Christians might add to our faith today.

Then ask your group to look up Ephesians 2:8-9 and list the steps Jesus asks us to take in order to be empowered and animated by him. Have students share their conclusions.

Step in the Right Direction Talksheet

Read Luke 11:37-54 and fill in the shoe prints with the kind of dance the Pharisees made people go through in order to be righteous. You can add to the list anything (not found in the Bible) that today's Christians might require of you in order to be righteous.

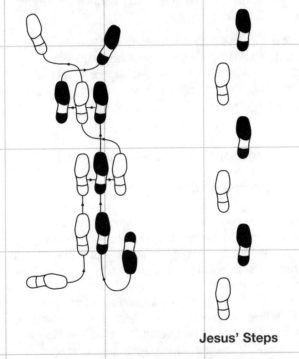

Jesus' Steps

Now read Ephesians 2:8-9 and fill in the shoe prints of Jesus with those things that would enable you to be empowered and animated by him.

Wrap Up

Idea #1: Ask your students to read Acts 17:28. Point out that this verse sums up what it means to have Christ live in us, fill us, and empower us. Invite your students to take a blank piece of paper and finish the following sentence: "What it means to me to 'live, move and have my being' in Christ is..." Close in prayer.

Idea #2: Ask your students to come up with a motto that describes the best way to live a Christian life free of all taint of legalism. (Have them read Acts 17:28 for a good example of one.) Close in prayer.

Production Notes: Step By Step 1

Producer: Javad Shadzi

I've never been a very good dancer, but sometimes I can't help but feel like I'm two-stepping through life, carefully placing my feet in the rhythm that life sets out for me. Sometimes, when life gets stressful, it's a provocative tango with the enemy. Or, when life is calm, it's a gentle waltz to the backdrop of an orchestra. When I look at the way I see my future, sometimes it feels like the Robot Dance—deliberate, forced, planned, and rigid. Robots don't move of their own will. Robots move in exactly the way they're programmed.

In a way we're all robots, programmed in the way we act, live, and think. Sometimes friends influence us, telling us that, in order to be accepted, we must act, think, or represent ourselves in a certain way. Other times it's parents who tell us this—

or MTV, teachers, employers, culture, etc. The Robot Dance is very tempting because it lures us into the false notion that if we can only live up to other people's expectations for our lives, we'll have fulfillment and acceptance.

I have to keep reminding myself that true fulfillment and acceptance only come from God, and it's his expectations that I need to live up to; it's his will that I need to seek. It's also tempting to think that living up to the expectations religion sets for us is truly living out God's will, but Jesus' admonishment of living by "the letter of the law" tells us otherwise.

The longer I dance, the more God shows me the moves I've made. Every once in a while, during a truly God-inspired moment, I look back on the freaky, busting moves I've made, choreographed by the Creator himself. Sweaty and with soaked wristbands, I groove to the cadence of the soul, moving in ways I don't understand, watching myself in slow motion, the organic beat of the universe pounding to the eternal rhythm of inspired love.

We often see the steps of our lives as formulated by others—our church, friends, society—but God wants us to dance life the way he created us to and in a way that is real, impassioned, defined in him, and powerful. Though others may not understand, they are moved and can't deny that the Creator of the universe energizes us.

Spin Cycle

2

4.99
WHITES
TRAINING
ORANGE CHICKEN
FRIED RICE

36 MINUT

FORTUN

PREP PRESENTATION

BULLET POINTS

Alternate Routes

 Emergent Ministries

Spin Cycle can be used as an illustration of being too busy for the important things in life. Another possible use is to make this clip a prelude to a moment of reflection with a well-placed word or two to set up the clip or by simply projecting the words of Jesus at the end of the show for a time of quiet prayer and meditation. (For example, Matthew 11:29: "Take my yoke upon you. Let me teach you, because I am humble and gentle, and you will find rest for your souls." NLT)

 Small Group

Focus: We must put God first in our lives and everything else in its proper perspective and order.

Biblical basis: Ecclesiastes 2:10-11, 4:4; Psalm 119:15-16

Stuff you need: *Spin Cycle* video, Bibles, discussion questions

Getting Started

Ask the students in your group to briefly describe their daily schedules. Depending on the age of your students, you may find that many of them are deeply committed to school, sports, and work, leaving little time for anything else. Ask them to rate how busy they are on a scale of one to 10, with 10 being very busy.

Transition to the *Spin Cycle* film clip by saying something like this:

> **Many of you already feel the weight of a super-busy life. Sometimes we tell ourselves that once we get a little older, we won't be so busy. But often this is not the case. Let's take a minute and watch a film clip that captures the sense of frustration that many people who are caught in a busy life start to feel, and then we'll discuss some alternatives to this lifestyle.**

▶ *Spin Cycle* Film Clip

Show *Spin Cycle* clip. When the film is over, ask your students to sum up—in one word—the feeling the movie is trying to convey.

Bible Study

Ask your students to read Ecclesiastes 2:10-11 and 4:4. Before they read, briefly give your students a vantage point for this book—a somewhat cynical observation of everything in life that ends with the writer coming to grips with what is really of substance and value: a relationship with God.

Discuss—

> * Do the words of this ancient writing ring true today?
>
> * How do you know when you have crossed the line from "working to live" to "living to work"? (For example, buying a car and then discovering that it takes all of your time and money to be able to keep it, so you rarely have time to use it.)

* Is there anything wrong with being very busy?

* Do you think you might have the tendency to become a workaholic? How would you know?

* We all know that being lazy is wrong, but is it just as wrong to be too busy?

* Describe a perfect balance among work, play, rest, socialization, and spiritual reflection.

* Who tends to be left out when our lives are too busy?

* If we are too busy with work, school, sports, etc., to give God our first or best attention, have we broken the first commandment?

Wrap Up

In a time of quiet reflection, ask your students to take a look at their lives and reevaluate their priorities. They should ask God if there are some places where cuts need to be made so they won't be too busy for him or for other things that will make their lives more well-rounded and balanced.

Close by reading these Psalm verses to your group: "I will study your commandments and reflect on your ways. I will delight in your principles and not forget your word." (Psalm 119:15-16, NLT)

Middle School

Focus: What's important and what's not.

Biblical basis: Luke 10:38-42

Stuff you need: A box full of all kinds of junk (small objects, nothing breakable), *Spin Cycle* video, Bibles, discussion questions, copies of *Spin Cycle* Talksheet, paper and pencils

Getting Started

Have your group sit in a circle. Tell them that the object of the game they are about to play is to keep from dropping what they are given.

Start by handing one person an object and telling her to pass it clockwise. Then hand a different object to another person and tell him to pass it counterclockwise. Keep doing this until you have a whole load of junk being passed around.

Sooner or later someone will end up not being able to control everything that is coming into his hands, and he will drop something. When this happens, this person is out of the game. You can either start again or simply keep the passing going until you are down to three people. The last two survivors win. (Let them take their pick of the junk as prizes.)

Transition to the *Spin Cycle* film clip by saying something like this:

> **This game shows how sometimes we can have more going on in our laps than we can handle. This short film clip we are about to watch does a good job of portraying this problem. Let's check it out.**

Spin Cycle

vol chp pg
04: 02: 29

▶ *Spin Cycle* Film Clip

Show the film clip. Transition to the Bible study by pointing out that all the people in the clip have very busy lives, and that maybe having a busy life is really just like having a washer stuck on the spin cycle—it doesn't accomplish the most important thing. Ask—

* What is the most important thing a washer must do?

* What is the most important thing we can do with our lives?

We're about to discover that.

Bible Study

Divide your students into groups of three or four and ask them to read the story of Mary and Martha found in Luke 10:38-42.

Assign each group at least one of the following methods to report to the whole group what they have read (and make sure to give them the needed materials to do so):

* Suppose a tabloid writer (like for the *National Enquirer*) was at this dinner and saw the interaction between Jesus and Martha. What kind of headlines do you think he would create about this event? Give us some examples.

* Draw a picture of Martha. Over her head create thought bubbles of what she might have been thinking when Mary never came back to help with the kitchen duties and sat

and listened to Jesus instead.

* Play the "devil's advocate" (someone who speaks up for the unpopular side) for Martha. Imagine you are a sympathetic friend who sides with her. Write down a few things you would say.

* Pretend you are with Miss Manners at this dinner. (Miss Manners answers letters from people wanting to know the proper thing to do in a particular situation.) Create a column that you think she would write for the newspaper outlining the proper behavior for a host and a guest. Decide for yourself if she would side with Jesus or Martha.

Ask your students to share what they have created.

Discuss these questions with your group—

* What is the moral—the bottom line idea—of this passage?

* According to Jesus, what is the best way people can spend their time and energy?

* How is this different from the way most people live their lives?

* The Bible is notably clear that God is to be put first. How can a person do this in everyday living?

* If it's not what we say but what we do that shows our real belief, what would you say about a person who seldom reads the Bible, seldom prays, etc., and the position God has in his or her life?

* What excuses do people give for not spending time focusing on God?

Wrap Up

Create a promise for your students to sign that reads something like this:

(or just go online and download the following Talksheet at www.YouthSpecialties.com/store/downloads; code: highway 4)

 I Promise Talksheet

I, _____, promise to spend more time reading the Bible and talking to God in order to put first things first in my life.

Hand out the promise sheets and point out that one way to put God first is to make it a point to always take time for him. Tell your students they do not have to make this promise, but that if they decide to sign this paper, it is a promise made to God to help them make sure they are putting first things first. Close in prayer.

High School

Focus: It's easy to get caught up doing things that don't matter and avoiding things that do. Wisdom comes from knowing the difference.

Biblical basis: Psalm 39:6-7; Matthew 6:25-34; Ecclesiastes

Stuff you need: paper, pencils, *Spin Cycle* video, Bibles, discussion questions, poster board, piles of magazines, scissors, and glue

Getting Started

Idea #1: Pass out paper and pencils to each student. Ask your students to work individually to chart their typical school day hour by hour—from waking to going to bed—listing what they normally do with their time. Ask them to look over what they have written and to evaluate if their lives are too busy, too full of free time, or just right. Poll your students to see what they say. (Results often vary with the age levels of students, but you might find that even in high school many kids see their lives as too busy.)

Transition to the *Spin Cycle* film clip by saying something like this:

> **We're given only one life to live, and
> many times people fill their days with so
> much of the mechanics of life that they
> don't really live—they feel they are on
> the spin cycle. Let's watch a short film
> clip that represents this idea.**

Show the clip and then transition to the Bible study by asking your students to listen carefully as you read these Psalm verses:

Spin Cycle

vol   chp   pg
04: 02: 33

We are merely moving shadows, and all our busy rushing ends in nothing. We heap up wealth for someone else to spend. And so, Lord, where do I put my hope? My only hope is in you. (Psalm 39:6-7, NLT)

Idea #2: Start your meeting by, without discussion or introduction, dimming the lights and showing the *Spin Cycle* film clip. After the show, ask your students—

> * What is the message of this short movie?

> * Do you think the people in the film are trapped?

> * How does a person know when she has crossed the line from "working to live" to "living to work"?

Transition to the Bible study by saying:—

Today we're going to take a look at some passages of Scripture that make no bones about the futility of putting all of our energy into things that, in the end, don't count and passages that point us toward things that do.

 ## Bible Study

Idea #1: Ask your students to break into groups of three or four and assign each one a chapter of Ecclesiastes to read. They should return to the larger group with a "report from the field" that gives this author's view on—

> * What hard work will bring

> * What money will do for you

* What pleasure has to offer

* What learning gets you

Before they read, briefly give your students a vantage point for this book—a somewhat cynical observation of everything in life that ends with the writer coming to grips with what is really of substance and value: a relationship with God.

After your groups report back, ask your students to give their feedback on these questions:

* Do you agree with the conclusions of Solomon, the writer of Ecclesiastes? Why or why not?

* What is our real duty based on Ecclesiastes 6:13?

* What is the first or the most important command that we are to obey?

* How do people get so busy that they break that command?

* What can people do to protect themselves from getting so caught up, even in good things, that they neglect the best thing: their relationship with God?

Idea #2: Break your group into groups of three or four and make sure everyone has access to a pile of magazines, scissors, glue, and poster board. Ask each group to read Ecclesiastes 2:1-11 and Matthew 6:25-34, then dig through the magazines for examples of things that can suck away your time, focus, and energy without giving you anything of real value in return. Instruct them to cut out all the images they can find, arrange them on their sheets of poster board, and then glue them down. Have your students share what they have posted on their boards and explain how those things can put us in the spin cycle but not give us real peace or purpose in life.

Wrap Up

Idea #1: Ask your students to design for themselves a balanced life. On blank pieces of paper have them write out what their day might look like if it were spent in a godly balance of doing the most important things that need to be done along with rest, socialization, and spiritual refreshment. Close in prayer, asking that God might grant these young people wisdom to follow this design.

Idea #2: Ask your students to evaluate their lives to see if there is one area where they need to make some adjustments so they don't fall into the spin cycle of life. Perhaps their lives are too busy and they need to drop something. Perhaps they need to rid themselves of something that owns them; perhaps they need to beef up their spiritual focus or use their time more wisely. Ask them to share that area with a partner for the sake of accountability and prayer. Close in prayer.

Production Notes: Spin Cycle

Director: Jonathan Green

However counter to my often-chaotic, right-brained way of thinking, a reliance on to-do lists has undoubtedly become one of the more dominant idiosyncrasies that I've inherited from my father. Generally speaking, I think it's a healthy practice—outlining the things you need to do and crossing them off as you complete each task. It's efficient, after all, and it feels so good to check things off. "Oh yeah, I put gas in the lawn mower—che-e-eck."

I do wonder, however, what effect this obsessive itemization has on our Palm Pilot-toting culture. We might be more efficient, but does that also make us more machine-like? Less human? Are we focused so intently on the fragments that we forget the whole? These were some of the questions that provoked me to make *Spin Cycle*. I decided to shoot the entire piece with a still camera, one frame at a time. This technique rendered the choppy, fragmented motion that I think best transmits the tension inherent in living our lives from one to-do item to the next.

That Guy

3

Small Group

Focus: Self-inspection

Biblical basis: Luke 5:1-8

Stuff you need: *That Guy* video, discussion questions, Bibles, paper and pencils

Getting Started

Ask your students to watch the humorous film clip *That Guy* with the idea not being, "I know some-one like that," but, "Gee, I wonder if I'm ever like that to someone?"

When the film is over, ask—

* Obviously, this over-the-top film shows the kind of guy who can bug the tar out of any-one, but do you have any habits or things you do that you *know* bug someone in your family or friendship circle? What is one of those things?

* Do you think people who are acting like jerks *know* they are being jerks? Why or why not?

* Some people think about themselves all the time—they are super self-conscious. Others never reflect on themselves or their own behavior at all. Do you think these atti-tudes affect how people behave?

* Why is it that we can usually see things about *others* that drive people nuts but we can't see those things in ourselves?

Transition to the Bible study by saying something like this:

Let's see if the Bible can help us avoid

being "that guy," as portrayed in the video, or at least help us to be honest enough to admit that we sometimes act like him.

 ## Bible Study

Ask your group to take a look at the situation in Luke 5:1-8. Discuss—

* What was Peter's job?

* Do you think Peter was skilled at his job?

* Do you suppose Peter thought he was a skilled fisherman?

* What do you think his attitude was when Jesus asked him to lower his nets once again?

* What does he realize about himself?

* If we all believed we were capable of being jerks sometimes, do you think it would make a difference in how we treat each other?

* Can you think of one way that you can be a jerk? (No, you don't have to share it if you don't want to.)

Wrap Up

Ask your students to write "The Jerk's Prayer"—an honest, open prayer to God from a person who realizes he has things in his life that bug him, just like other people do. Ask the students to share what they've written and then close by reading a few of these prayers aloud.

Focus: The secret of wise behavior. Being "that guy" can, in part, be avoided.

Biblical basis: James 1:23-24, 26; Proverbs 1:7; 3:27-28, 30; 10:5, 8-9, 12, 19; 11:13, 17, 24; 12:18; 14:7-8, 15, 17, 22; 16:3; 17:14; 1 John 1:9

Stuff you need: *That Guy* video, discussion questions, whiteboard or overhead and something to write with, Bibles, paper and pencils

Getting Started

Start your meeting by showing the *That Guy* clip without comment to your group. When the film is over, ask—

> * Do you know anybody who is like that guy? (Watch for them to point all over the room on this question.)
>
> * Do you think anybody ever sees *you* as that guy? Why or why not?

Transition to the Bible study by saying something like this:

> **The Bible gives us some practical advice on how not to be a jerk—and even some on what to do if we think we never act like one. Let's take a look at some of it.**

 Bible Study

Pass out paper and pencils to your students. Ask them to get into groups of three or four, and tell them to fold their paper in half to make a book. Tell them they are going to write "the book" on how *not* to be that guy, based on the passages of Scripture they are given. (They can use as many pages as they need.)

On a whiteboard or overhead write the following verses (you can add more if you like):

JAMES 1:23-24
JAMES 1:26
PROVERBS 1:7
PROVERBS 3:27-28
PROVERBS 3:30
PROVERBS 10:5
PROVERBS 10:8
PROVERBS 10:9
PROVERBS 10:12
PROVERBS 10:19
PROVERBS 11:13
PROVERBS 11:17
PROVERBS 11:24
PROVERBS 12:18
PROVERBS 14:7
PROVERBS 14:8
PROVERBS 14:15
PROVERBS 14:17
PROVERBS 14:22
PROVERBS 16:3
PROVERBS 17:14
"AND IF WE FIND OURSELVES BEING JERKS…" 1 JOHN 1:9

Your students should read the passages, put them into their own words, and then write these bits of advice inside their books. Ask your students to share what they have "published."

Wrap Up

Ask your students to think of one person they know who, if asked, would be willing to level with

them about how they act. Ask students to invite
that person to tell them if they are doing things
that put them in the "jerk" or "annoying" category.
Close in prayer.

 High School

Focus: We need to recognize that we sometimes annoy others and learn to forgive those who annoy us.

Biblical basis: Proverbs 12:15; 19:11; 21:4; 22:15; Jeremiah 17:9;
Mark 7:21; James 2:13; Luke 6:37; 1 Thessalonians
5:14; Romans 12:8, 16

Stuff you need: a mirror, discussion questions, *That Guy* video, paper,
pencils, copies of a personality quiz or copies of That
Guy Talksheet, prescription pads (optional), 3x5 cards

Getting Started

Idea #1:

Grab a mirror and hold it up in front of your group.
Ask—

* What is good and bad about a mirror? *(It tells
the truth.)*

* How could you avoid the truth of the mirror?
(Avoid the mirror; say the mirror is lying.)

* As disturbing as the truth of the mirror can be,
are we better off with it or without it? Why?

Transition to the film clip by saying something like
this:

**We are going to watch a short, goofy
film clip that is intended to give us a
message: As obnoxious as the guy in**

the film is—sometimes we are that guy!

Show *That Guy* film clip to your group. Afterward, roll into the Bible study by saying something like this:

> **As much as we don't like to admit it, there are things about us that can drive other people nuts.**

Idea #2: Ask your students to pair off with a friend. Each person should make a list of five of their own habits, traits, or tendencies that they know can annoy their friends or family members. For example, the tendency to procrastinate can cause them to pull a last-minute all-nighter to finish a term paper, or perhaps they have a habit of leaving "crumbs" (such as empty soda cans, candy wrappers, and other trash) wherever they go. Ask your group to share what they've heard from their friends.

Transition to the *That Guy* film clip by saying something like this:

> **If we're honest, there are things about all of us that can drive other people nuts. We tend to see them as small, "so what?" kinds of habits or traits. But what if we are more annoying than we think—what if we are "that guy"?**

Roll the clip.

 ## Bible Study

Idea #1: After the film clip, ask your students—Do you know anyone like that? (Kids will probably chime in with a name or two.) Point out that in some situations *we* may be that guy! Then explain that annoyance is a two-pronged problem. It involves—

1. Coming to grips with the realization that each of us has the potential to be a plague to someone else, and

2. Controlling our reactions toward those people who bug us.

In order to address these two ideas, divide your group in half and hand out paper and pencils. Then assign the groups the following Scripture passages and give them these instructions.

Group 1—Your job is to gaze in the mirror and see if you can come up with an honest assessment of what each one of us as a human being is *really* like—not based on our own wishful thinking or the slick propaganda of the media, but on the truths of the Bible. Please read the following passages: Proverbs 12:15; 21:4; 22:15; Jeremiah 17:9; Mark 7:21; and Romans 12:16. When you come across a human trait, list it on your paper and then illustrate how this trait would show up among typical students your age. Keep in mind that the example doesn't have to be horrific—just annoying. You may choose to share your examples with the other group in written form, as drawings, acted out, or expressed in any other creative way you wish.

Group 2—Since you know we will never escape "that guy," your job is to develop a game plan for how to handle the annoying people you will meet, work with—and, yes, probably marry. Read the following passages and come up with an example from everyday life that shows how to put this idea into action: Proverbs 19:11; James 2:13; Luke 6:37; 1 Thessalonians 5:14; and Romans 12:8. Your examples can be written, drawn, acted out, or expressed in any other creative way you wish.

Have your students share what they have discovered.

Idea #2: Help your students realize how their personalities can clash with the personalities of others. One way to do this is by giving them a quickie personality test (like the one Gary Smalley created, which uses Lion, Otter, Golden Retriever, and Beaver types). After they've taken the test, interpret the results with them and make comparisons between the different personality types. Ask for a show of hands for each personality type and have the students look around so they can see that not everyone in the group has the same personality.

You can also use the fun (but not terribly professional) "The Walk in the Woods" talksheet (see the Talksheet download at www.YouthSpecialties.com/store/downloads; code: highway 4). If you do so, it would probably work best to have students pair off and say their choices to each other first, then report back to the whole group *after* they've completed the profile. During the group sharing time, pause after reading each sentence and ask a few volunteers to read their descriptions. Then read the explanation from the leader's Response Key below. The results are often pretty funny.

The Walk in the Woods Talksheet

Read the narrative and write down what you would do at each point.

You are walking on a trail when you come to a forest. Describe the forest and say what you feel and do in relationship to it (e.g., Are you scared? Apprehensive? Happy? Do you enter or not?).

You do enter the forest. Along the path you find a key. Describe the key and tell what you do with it.

Next you come upon a cup. Describe the cup and tell what you do with it.

You come upon a body of water. Describe the body of water and tell what you do in relationship to it.

You come upon a bear. Describe the bear and tell what you do in relationship to it.

You come upon a wall. Describe the wall and tell what you do in relationship to it.

Response Key (for the leader's eyes only)

The forest represents the individual's outlook on life,

the key represents the individual's outlook on education,

the cup represents the individual's outlook on religion,

the water represents the individual's outlook on sex,

the bear represents the individual's outlook on problems or trouble,

and the wall represents the individual's outlook on death.

When your students have finished comparing their personalities or perspectives on life's big issues, ask them to look up Jeremiah 17:9 and Mark 7:21, which point out the nature of the human condition. Introduce the passages with a comment such as—

In addition to being very different from each other, if you factor in some of the elements from these verses, we humans can be quite annoying to each other.

Then say:

The overarching question is what do we do when people bug us? Please get into pairs and read the following passages: Proverbs 19:11; James 2:13; Luke 6:37; 1 Thessalonians 5:14; and Romans 12:8. Then work together to write the "Great Physician's" prescription for handling the plague known as "fellow humans."

If you can, make up some blank prescription pads for this part of the session—it adds to the fun. Ask your group to share what they have prescribed.

Wrap Up

Idea #1: Ask each student to think of one person who really drives her nuts. Challenge her to make it a private matter of prayer and effort to forgive the person, have patience with him, and create an atmosphere of peace with him. Ask for a few minutes of silence and meditation as your students prepare their hearts to deal with "that guy" in more appropriate ways.

Idea #2: Ask your students to weigh whether or not—in *some* way—they are "that guy" in the life of someone else. Ask them to identify one of their own annoying behaviors, traits, or habits that they could begin to work on this week. Invite each of them to write that habit or tendency on a 3x5 card or slip of paper—but without their names. Then collect the cards and tell your students that you intend to pray about what they've anonymously written, asking God to help take the edge off some of their foibles. Close in prayer.

Production Notes: That Guy

Producer/Cinematographer:
Ryan Pettey

Like the Highlander, he has existed in every culture through the centuries. He has taken on many forms, showed himself in the most remote locations, and challenged cultural mores across the globe. He is "That Guy," the necessary cornerstone of every society. Although donning the responsibilities of "That Guy" is no small task, a handful have gratefully accepted the duty. That Guy shows us that it is possible to find belonging and meaning while fulfilling a role we believe the community calls us to fill—no matter how challenging it may be. What would you do when faced with a true calling? Would you run or would you accept your role within the body? Would you be THAT GUY?

JoeNineEleven

4

Alternate Routes

 General Church Use

You won't find a much better film clip to use than this one when the subject is priorities or God moving despite horrible circumstances. This is also a powerful clip to use on the anniversary of the events of 9/11/2001.

 Emergent Ministries

9/11 was a national tragedy that has been burned into the minds of all American citizens. This short piece by a survivor is a stark, sobering bit of testimony to the brevity of life, the necessity of reexamining our priorities, and the presence of God in the midst of horror—a strong bit of work when you are looking for a reflective moment. You may want to preface or end this piece by reading or projecting Psalm 27:5-6:

> For in the day of trouble he will keep me safe in his dwelling; he will hide me in the shelter of his tabernacle and set me high upon a rock. Then my head will be exalted above the enemies who surround me.

Small Group

Focus: The values we have when facing death are those we should have in life.

Biblical basis: James 4:14; 1 Peter 1:24

Stuff you need: *JoeNineEleven* video, discussion questions, Bibles, paper and pencils

Getting Started

Ask your students to share where they were when they first heard about 9/11 and what their thoughts, emotions, and feelings were as the disaster unfolded. No doubt many of your students were powerfully affected by what they saw and heard that morning.

Transition into the film clip *JoeNineEleven* by saying something like this:

> **Imagine what it must have been like to be in the World Trade Center that September morning. Let's watch a short film featuring a man who found himself on the ninth floor of Tower 1. Listen carefully to see if you can pick up the changes in his perspective.**

Show the film clip.

 ## Bible Study

Involve your group in a discussion about what they have just seen and heard in the film by asking questions such as—

* How do you think you would feel if you survived an attack like this but watched others—alive but unable to escape—leap to their deaths?

* What would you say Joe's priorities were before 9/11?

* How about after 9/11?

* From Joe's story, it's obvious that he thought he was going to die when the dust from the Trade Center began to choke him. What do you think of his description of calm and letting go at that point?

* What kinds of questions might go through your mind if you were to survive something like this?

* What does this say to you about the brevity of life?

Ask your group to look up James 4:14 and 1 Peter 1:24 and discuss how quickly and unexpectedly life can end. Ask questions such as—

* When someone knows he is about to die, what values do you think he holds?

* How do these values differ from those of someone who may not think a whit about death?

* How might a person's life be different if she chose to live by the values she would hold at the point of death?

Wrap Up

Ask your group to imagine they are trapped on the top floor of Tower 1. They have only a few minutes to write a final note to their loved ones and to tell their friends what is important in life before sailing the note off the tower in hopes that it will be found after their deaths. Pass out paper and pencils and give your students a brief moment to jot down some ideas. Ask a few to share their notes and then encourage your group to begin to live by those values today. Close in prayer.

 Middle School

Focus: God will see us through incredible hardships.

Biblical basis: 2 Corinthians 11:24-27; Romans 8:38-39

Stuff you need: discussion questions, *JoeNineEleven* video, Bibles, large sheets of newsprint, art supplies, paper and pencils, clay, digital camera

Getting Started

The 9/11 tragedy was an event that took place during the childhood of your middle school students. For this film clip to be relevant you may need to review some of the details for those who have a sketchy memory of the event. Start with a few discussion questions such as—

* What do people mean when they say 9/11?

* What exactly happened on that day?

* Who flew the planes and for what reason?

* About how many people were killed on that day?

* What would you have done if you were one of the people stuck on the upper floors of the World Trade Center? Would you have jumped rather than be burned or crushed?

* What do you remember feeling or thinking on September 11, 2001?

Transition to the lesson by saying something like this:

> **Today we are going to watch a film clip featuring a man who was in Tower 1 when terrorists flew a hijacked jet plane into its upper floors. As you listen to his reflections on this event, see if you can hear any changes in Joe's thinking as a result of what he experienced.**

Play the *JoeNineEleven* film clip. Then slide into the Bible study by saying something like this:

> **Disasters are not something new— these kind of stories are recorded in the Bible. It's not the disasters but how we *respond* to them that matters most in the end. Let's take a look at some examples from God's Word.**

 ## Bible Study

Divide your students into groups of four to six and ask them to read 2 Corinthians 11:24-27. After giving them a bit of background information on the Apostle Paul, assign each group one of the following activities (and make sure to give them the needed materials to do so):

* Create a mural showing the various hardships Paul went through.

* Based on this passage write entry pages in Paul's journal describing what happened to him. Take artistic liberties with dates and details.

* Create a coat of arms that might represent Paul and the hardships he endured.

* Make a slide show of Paul's hardships using clay figures and a digital camera to capture each situation.

* Design a résumé for Paul listing his qualifications to endure hard times.

* Imagine that Paul carried a briefcase with him. Create an ad for that briefcase based on the hardships Paul might have dragged it through.

Ask the groups to share what they've created. Then read Romans 8:38-39 to your students.

Now take a minute and ask your students to help you create a list of hardships that kids their age face. When you're finished, compare the lists. No doubt the stuff Paul went through was much tougher to endure than what most kids experience. Take a few moments to discuss Paul's attitude toward his hardships.

Wrap Up

Ask your students to compose a prayer for those who are facing difficult moments. Read the various prayers and invite students who might secretly be having a rough time to make those prayers their own.

High School

Focus: Getting our priorities right

Biblical basis: Luke 10:38-42; Matthew 6:33; 2 Chronicles 1:11-12

Stuff you need: a picture of the World Trade Center twin towers before they were hit on 9/11, *JoeNineEleven* video, Bibles, paper and pencils, discussion questions

Getting Started

Idea #1: Ask your students to share a memory they will never forget. You may get a wide variety of answers on this first pass. Then ask your students to share a memory of a day they will always remember. This time you may be more likely to have someone refer to 9/11. If not, ask, "What about 9/11?" Take a few minutes to let your kids discuss where they were and what they were thinking on that day.

Transition to the clip by saying something like this:

> **Today we are going to watch a film clip of a man who was working in Tower 1 when the first jet slammed into it. Let's see and hear his reflections of that moment and what we can learn from his story.**

Show the film clip.

Idea #2: Before the meeting, go online and see if you can find a picture of the New York skyline that shows the twin towers. Print it out and pin it on a board. Now show the image to your students and ask—What's wrong with this picture? It shouldn't take more than a moment for someone to point

out that the twin towers are no longer standing.
Begin a discussion about where your students
were on that day, what their thoughts and fears
might have been, and how they feel about it now.

Transition to the clip by telling your students—

> **Today we are going to watch a short
> movie where a survivor reflects on that
> disaster. Listen carefully to see if you
> can pick up the difference that surviving
> such a horror has made in his life.**

 ## Bible Study

Idea #1: Using Joe's comments as a starting
point, ask your students to work in pairs to come
up with a short list of things that are truly important in life (give them paper and pencils to use as
they do this). Guide them toward these Scriptures
to help with the process: Luke 10:38-42; Matthew
6:33; 2 Chronicles 1:11-12. Ask your pairs to come
up with some examples from everyday life of how
those priorities could look in action. Have your students share what they have written.

Idea #2: Discuss the contents of the film clip. Use
discussion question such as—

> * How do you think you would feel if you sur-
> vived an attack like this but watched others,
> alive but unable to escape, leap to their
> deaths?
>
> * What would you say Joe's priorities were
> before 9/11?
>
> * How about after 9/11?

* From Joe's story, it's obvious that he thought he was going to die when the dust from the Trade Center began to choke him. What do you think of his description of calm and letting go at that point?

* What kinds of questions might go through your mind if you were to survive something like this?

* What kinds of changes might take place in your life? (Discuss the change in priorities that a near-death event like this can bring to someone's life.)

Remind your students that the values we have when facing death are those we should have in life.

Now have your students read the following passages and work in small groups to come up with a "Bill of What's Right"—a document that lists the types of priorities that people in God's kingdom ought to have: Luke 10:38-42; Matthew 6:33; 2 Chronicles 1:11-12. Ask the groups to share what they have written and discuss how these priorities might work out in everyday living.

Wrap Up

Idea #1: Ask your students to come up with one thing in their lives that needs to be reprioritized. Ask them to write on a slip of paper what they will attempt to do to put that area back in line with God's order. Suggest that they trade slips with a trustworthy friend who will commit to pray for them concerning this area of their life and who will keep their confidence. Close in prayer.

Idea #2: If you used Bible study idea #2, have

willing students prayerfully sign the "Bill of What's Right" as a symbol of their desire to put first things first in the way they live their lives. Close in prayer.

 ## Production Notes: JoeNineEleven

Producer/Cinematographer: Joe Perez

Joe Viscuglia, a 9/11 survivor, contacted us with his incredible story that needed to be told. We were all huddled around a coffee table in the Red Rock Café when I first heard it. With preconceptions about what the story was going to be (and since it had been almost two-and-a-half years after the events occurred), I thought to myself, *How are we going to pull off a 9/11 story without the loss of interest from viewers who have been told the general story thousands of times already?*

He started telling the story, and right away we were captivated by his words. Near the end I started welling with emotion, not caused by the literal story that he was telling but by the realization he'd had as a *result* of that story. Sure, I was sad and amazed at hearing about the horrific happenings of 9/11, but for someone to experience a total transformation in his life as a result of them is truly moving—a movement toward my own inward transformation.

Consequences

5

what is
the

Alternate Route

Emergent Ministries

Use this little clip to illustrate the fact that regardless of how adrift people in our culture are from their moral moorings, God is still at work in their hearts, bringing a sense of remorse (or guilt) when they disobey him.

Small Group

Focus: The consequence of remorse can be God's gift to us.

Biblical basis: Genesis 3:1-24; 2 Samuel 12:1-14; Deuteronomy 32:48-52; 1 Samuel 2:27-31; Acts 5:1-10; Galatians 6:7

Stuff you need: discussion questions, *Consequences* video, Bibles, paper and pencils

Getting Started

Ask your students to give you a definition of *guilt*. Discuss these questions—

* Where does it come from?

* How does it affect us?

Transition to the *Consequences* film clip by saying something like this:

Let's watch a short film where, in a

man-on-the-street interview style, people tell an interviewer their thoughts about what happens when they knowingly do wrong rather than right.

▶ *Consequences* Film Clip

Show the clip and then discuss the various comments and reactions people in the film had about the emotion of guilt.

 Bible Study

Select one of the following biblical case studies that show how disobedience often comes with a heavy price tag of consequences:

Genesis 3:1-24—Adam and Eve

2 Samuel 12:1-14—David and Bathsheba

Deuteronomy 32:48-52—Moses and the Promised Land

1 Samuel 2:27-31—Eli and his sons

Acts 5:1-10—Ananias and Sapphira

As a group, read the account you have selected and then discuss where the individual(s) went wrong and the results. Discuss consequences in the light of Galatians 6:7—reaping what we sow. Ask—

Why, in most cases, do you think guilt might be a "gift" from God or part of his loving design?

Wrap Up

Hand out paper and pencils and ask your students to dream up a "Stop, look, and listen" type of motto that people can recall when they're tempted by situations with potentially bad consequences. Close in prayer.

 Middle School

Focus: Disobeying God brings lousy consequences.

Biblical basis: Genesis 3:1-24; 2 Samuel 12:1-14; Deuteronomy 32:48-52; 1 Samuel 2:27-31; Acts 5:1-10; 1 John 1:9

Stuff you need: checkerboards, checkers or other small game pieces, consequence slips from the Consequences Talksheet, and a paper sack for each pair of students

Getting Started

Reproduce the "Consequences" talksheet and cut it into slips. Make up a small paper sack of cut-up slips for each pair of students. You can also make paper checkerboards if you have a lot of kids.

Divide your students into pairs and give each twosome a checkerboard and checkers. (If you made your own paper checkerboards, you can use buttons or another small item for game pieces instead.) Tell your kids that this is a game of "Consequence Checkers." If they lose a game piece, they have to reach into the sack of consequences, pull out a slip of paper, and complete the action. Naturally, the better player a person is, the fewer consequences he will have to draw and complete. All consequences MUST be paid. Let your students play. (You may want to give them a time limit and let the one who has the most pieces left be the winner.)

Here is a list of the consequences found on the talksheet (you can download the Talksheet at www.YouthSpecialties.com/store/downloads; code: highway 4). You can make up your own as well.

Consequence Checkers Talksheet

Do 10 push-ups.

Hold your breath for one minute.

Sing the national anthem.

Rub your stomach and pat your head.

Crow like a rooster.

Suck your thumb while saying, "Goo-goo."

Say out loud, "Does my breath smell like dog food?"

Hop on one foot for 30 seconds.

Spin in a circle 10 times and whistle.

Put your shoes on the wrong feet.

Smell your armpit and say, "Phew!"

Pretend to pick lice from your hair.

Imitate a cartoon character.

Do a ballerina move across the floor.

Write your name while holding a pen with your toe.

Sing a jingle from a TV commercial.

Pretend you are Santa Claus.

Ask someone if your knees are too big.

Try to put your foot behind your head.

Grab your ankles and walk around quacking like a duck.

Sing the "Alphabet Song."

Howl like a coyote.

Make kissing noises.

Transition to the film clip by saying something like this:

Consequences are part of life. They can be silly, as in this game; they can be good, like getting an A on a report card for hard work; or they can be bad. God places in each one of us a sense of good and bad, right and wrong, and some kind of conscience to help us know which is which. Let's take a look at a man-on-the-street interview that talks about this and the consequences of not paying attention to that little voice inside.

▶ *Consequences* **Film Clip**

Play the *Consequences* clip. Recap briefly what was being said in the film.

Bible Study

Divide your students into groups of three or four and assign each of them at least one of the following passages: Genesis 3:1-24; 2 Samuel 12:1-14; Deuteronomy 32:48-52; 1 Samuel 2:27-31; or Acts 5:1-10. Instruct them to act like a detective agency and locate three things in each Scripture passage:

* Who was involved in this situation

* Where the individual failed to do what was right

* The consequence of that failure

Ask the groups to report what they discover. Now remind your students that the Bible is also filled with examples of good consequences. Joshua, Daniel, and Joseph—to name a few—all listened to what God put in their hearts and obeyed.

Ask—

* What do you feel when you go against what you know to be right? (Most will say guilt.)

* How does a person get rid of guilt?

Wrap Up

Invite your students to memorize 1 John 1:9 as the key to end the pain of a guilty conscience. Close in prayer.

Middle School

Focus: Consequences, both good and bad, are marks of God's love and concern for us.

Biblical basis: Genesis 3:1-24; 2 Samuel 12:1-14; Deuteronomy 32:48-52; 1 Samuel 2:27-31; Acts 5:1-10; Galatians 6:7

Stuff you need: *Consequences* video, a college diploma (optional), discussion questions, Bibles, video cameras, paper and pencils, copies of Consequences Talksheets

Getting Started

Idea #1: Have your students do a call and response for behavior and consequences. You call out a behavior and have your group kick back a consequence response. Try some of these for starters (you can add more to these if you like):

Don't brush and floss

Do your homework

Cheat on your girlfriend or boyfriend

Don't wear a seat belt

Write thank-you notes to people who give you stuff

Spend too much time in the sun

Smoke

Save yourself sexually until marriage

Transition to the film clip by saying something like this:

We live in a world where our actions have consequences—good or bad. Let's see what happens during a man-on-the-street interview when rank-and-file citi-

zens are asked about their behavior and
the results of it.

Show the *Consequences* clip.

Idea #2: Bring in a college diploma (yours or
someone else's, like a doctor's). Ask your students
to give you some feedback about the consequences of that piece of paper:

* What were the economic consequences of
  acquiring it?

* What were the time consequences of getting it?

* What are the life consequences of having it?

* What might the consequences be without it?

Point out to your students that a college degree is
not handed out lightly—it must be *earned*. The
degree is an example of a good consequence, but
there are other examples of the opposite.

Transition to the film clip by saying something like
this:

> We live in a world where our actions
> have consequences—good or bad. Let's
> see what happens during a man-on-the-
> street interview when rank-and-file citi-
> zens are asked about their behavior and
> the results of it.

Show the *Consequences* clip and afterward discuss the interviewees' reactions to their own personal moral failures. Ask—

* Do some of these people seem a bit clueless as to why they feel guilt?

* What do you think guilt is?

* Why/how might guilt be considered a good consequence for doing wrong?

Transition to the Bible study by saying something like—

The Bible is full of examples of what happens when we violate what we know to be right. Let's take a look at a few of those situations.

 ## Bible Study

Idea #1: Read Galatians 6:7 to your students and then ask them to break up into groups of three or four and assign each group at least one of the following case studies:

Genesis 3:1-24—Adam and Eve

2 Samuel 12:1-14—David and Bathsheba

Deuteronomy 32:48-52—Moses and the Promised Land

1 Samuel 2:27-31—Eli and his sons

Acts 5:1-10—Ananias and Sapphira

Working with their groups, students should read their assigned biblical example and then see if they can put the same type of failure into a modern story or example. When the students finish, have them share their updated versions.

Spend a short time discussing the following questions:

  * Why do you think people do what they know is wrong?

  * Why do some people, knowing the likelihood of bad consequences, continue what they're doing?

  * How do you process making a decision about right and wrong? Do consequences come into play?

Idea #2: After watching the *Consequences* film clip with your students, spend a little time debriefing with questions such as—

  * What do you think the conscience is?

  * Do you think unbelievers know the difference between right and wrong? Why or why not?

  * Someone once said that guilt is like an acid—it eventually burns through anything put in front of it to block it. Do you agree with this description? Why or why not?

  * Why do you think people do what they know is wrong?

  * Why do some people continue what they're doing even when they know there's a likelihood of bad consequences?

  * How do you process making a decision about right and wrong? Do consequences come into play?

  * Do you think guilt is a good thing or a bad thing? Why?

Break the students into groups of two or three. Give your students video cameras or notepads and pencils to use and send them out into the foyer of the church, the mall, or wherever is handy, to do a little man-on-the-street interviewing of their own. Have them approach strangers, let them know they are doing a research project, and ask if they would answer a couple of questions. You can use these questions or make up your own:

* Have you ever changed a behavior because of a bad consequence?

* Do you ever feel guilty?

* What do you do when you feel guilty?

* Where do you think a sense of guilt for wrong behavior comes from?

Coach your students to be polite and courteous. Give them a time limit.

When the groups return, have them make a report about the answers they received. Discuss people's responses.

Now direct your students to Galatians 6:7. Ask them to comment on the wisdom of this passage in everyday life.

Wrap Up

Idea #1: Share with your students that God promises forgiveness of sin, but he never promises deliverance from the consequences of sin. Pass out paper and pencils to your students and ask them to draw a picture of an old-fashioned set of scales or balance on the paper. (You can also download a Talksheet with a picture of a scale on it from www.YouthSpecialties.com/store/downloads; code: highway 4.)

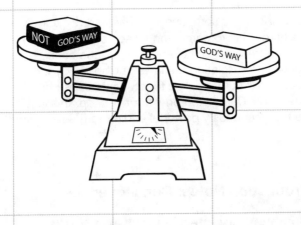

Using the scale as a symbol of some issue about which they could make a good or bad decision (such as sexual activity, honesty, personal industry, reading the Bible, etc.), your students can work individually to list on one side of the scale the possible consequences of tipping God's way and on the other side the possible consequences of tipping the scale away from what God would desire.

Encourage your students to mentally go through this process each time they come to a crossroads of decision in their lives. Close in prayer.

Idea #2: Invite someone who has had to "learn the hard way" to come and close your meeting by sharing the story of how he suffered the consequences for violating the laws of God. Ask your guest if it would be okay for students to ask him questions. Depending on whom you tap, this can be a tremendously powerful ending to the session.

 ## Production Notes: Consequences

Documentary Interviewer: Kevin Marks

Christians always talk to each other about God's will. If you hang around church groups long enough, you know what that phrase means— God's personal plan for your own life. Christians are always asking themselves if they're "inside God's will" (i.e., "God, is it your will that I find my car keys? I'm late!"). We know God has a will for everyone—not just Christians—and we wanted to talk to people on the street about it. The trouble is, most people don't recognize the phrase "God's will." People do, however, describe something called the conscience—that little voice of morality or that internal instinct that nudges them this way or that.

Joe and I hit a few coffeehouses and asked some college students if they had ever done anything contrary to what their conscience was telling them, and if so, how did it feel? The answers are about what you'd expect—they felt bad and like they had cheated themselves. (Except, of course, for the brave few who seem to go through life operating with no conscience whatsoever.)

The fascinating thing is that what these folks describe as their little internal battle with their con-sciences just might be their own supernatural struggles with the Creator, even though they're describing it using very non-sacred language. Does God care enough about everyone, Christian and not, to speak into their lives with a small inter-nal voice, guiding them in how to act, what to think, and what to do? It's possible. If so, we'd like to thank him for operating on the conscience of the staff of Coffee Society in Cupertino, California. They let us film in their fine shop for a good hour or so and never threatened to kick us out.

HIGHWAY VISUAL CURRICULUM
WHAT DO YOU WANT?
UNDERSTANDING GOD'S WILL

Life is often presented to students as "predestined," that God has this perfect plan for us, and all we have to do is figure out God's will and align ourselves with that. Every choice from whether you go to college in Boston or San Diego to whether you super size your meal is presented as an opportunity to find God's will. The Church has romanticized the reality of God's will, making it unrealistic: defining something that only God can define.

Our faith in God is the same way. God wills us to live "in him," wherever, with the life we have, in whatever we're doing ... there is no place where God is not, and there is nothing we can do (with true intentions) where God can't lead, transform, and manifest. How absurd is it, that we wait for God's will to be revealed ... waiting until circumstances coincide with OUR will?

Highway Visual Curriculum gives you the tools to help your students with life. By focusing on issues, and using compelling video segments and a unique leader's guide, this DVD package will help you lead your students through the ride.

The WHAT DO YOU WANT? curriculum
Each of the five lessons contains sections to help you customize material for middle school, high school, and even general church use. Five unforgettable productions—dramas, comedies, interviews, music videos, documentary/mockumentary formats—are biblically based with practical application-points.

Highway Video is a band of visual creatives, based in Northern California, who have experienced the spiritual power of visual expression. Highway produces media pieces used by those in worship and ministry to engage people in real places with God. Curriculum writer **Rick Bundschuh** is a veteran youth worker, author, cartoonist, and teaching pastor of Kauai Christian Fellowship in Hawaii.

 Build your **Highway Visual Curriculum Library!**
Look for other DVD packages in the series!

 Features: **downloadable worksheets** in multiple formats, customizable for your use; web links; and more!

CHURCH AND MINISTRY / CHURCH LIFE / EVANGELISM & OUTREAC

ISBN 0-310-25834-0